Finding Your Keys

ISBN: 979-8-9850634-0-0

The Keys

are the property of:

____

(Your Name)

Introduction:

Through self reflection and discovery, this workbook journal, rooted in faith, is designed to help you discover "KEYS" that will unlock the path to your happiness and peace. You will explore the role communication and validation play in helping you find your Keys.

Through communication, you find validation in others approval and feedback. The process of discovering your Keys explores how you interact and respond to people in your daily life; It is designed to remind you that, "You hold the Keys to how **YOU** show up in your life and how people interact and receive you".

As you begin to process your thoughts and feelings through this process, first ask yourself these questions:

- Am I an effective communicator? *Yes / No*
- Have I surrendered my communication power to others? *Often / Sometimes / Never*
- Do I provide others the ability to lock or unlock my happiness and peace? *Yes / No / Maybe*

This process will also explore how you receive and seek validation from others.

This journey will prompt you to answer the questions:
1. Are my choices bringing me happiness and peace?
2. Do the choices I make aid in the advancement of other's success, their survival and happiness ahead of my own?

My desire is for you to recognize when you have lost the Keys to your own happiness and peace.

Throughout this book, I have infused thoughts I refer to as, *"In The Keys of Life"*. These are lessons life has taught me as I have traveled on my journey. I hope *"In the Keys of Life"* will inspire you to think about your own experiences, the lessons you've learned along the way and how these lessons unlocked your path to happiness and peace.

You have to put in the work to reap the highest reward for *yourself.* This is not a journey for you if you are not ready to invest the time over the next 30 days.

It requires a true commitment to objective self-evaluation, growth and a willingness to develop and put into motion **YOUR** plan of action. As you travel this path and reach different levels of awareness, you will find the Keys that will unlock the doors for you to begin living your BEST LIFE.

God gave you the KEYS to unlock your destiny. Be still, focus on that which He has given only to you. Know that you have the power to reclaim all that He has written for you. His blueprint is clear and His reward is Great! It's yours for the taking, just call upon Him for direction and clarity as you start this journey to find and reclaim your Keys.

In the back of this book you will find reference materials (reading options and a definition of terms) to help you on your journey.

I wish you
Peace, Blessings and Love,
Nicole

PROVERBS 4:13 (NIV)

HOLD ON TO INSTRUCTION, DO NOT LET IT GO; GUARD IT WELL, FOR IT IS YOUR LIFE.

The journal

The journal is designed to be thought provoking and to trigger contemplation over the next 30 days. After you complete each segment (Communication, Validation, Happiness & Peace), capstone assignments are available to mark the completion of each section. Completing each section of the journal will lead to discovering Keys to happiness and peace. Meditate and reflect quietly on how you are feeling frequently during this journey.

Begin Day 1 of this journal on a Saturday. Schedule time to complete one activity per day. Journal your thoughts and feelings during this process in the "My Thoughts" journal. Space is available at the end of each section for you to take notes for subsequent reflection. The journal has six opportunities (sections) for you to develop Keys and a final entry to secure your Keys. They will help you document and organize your feelings:

Self Reflective Journaling Opportunities:
Self Evaluation Work Entries - For your Consideration
Your Personal Journal - My Thoughts (keep a personal journal)

Bullet Journal Entry Opportunities:
Saturday Cool down - Rest, Stop, Review
Sunday Summary - The Week That Was
Segment Summary Pt. 1 - Key Finding Capstone - 5 Points
Segment Summary Pt. 2 - Key Finding Capstone - My Keys
Securing Your Keys - The final exercise - The Lockbox Passcode

= you've reached the end of the days journal exercise
Make the commitment and enjoy the journey
as you find your Keys to Happiness and Peace

Self-Reflection

Day 1 part 1. FOR YOUR CONSIDERATION

Today is the first day of your journey. Log what you feel your strengths and weaknesses are in each area.

List the personal Keys you hope to develop over the next 30 days.

Communication

Validation

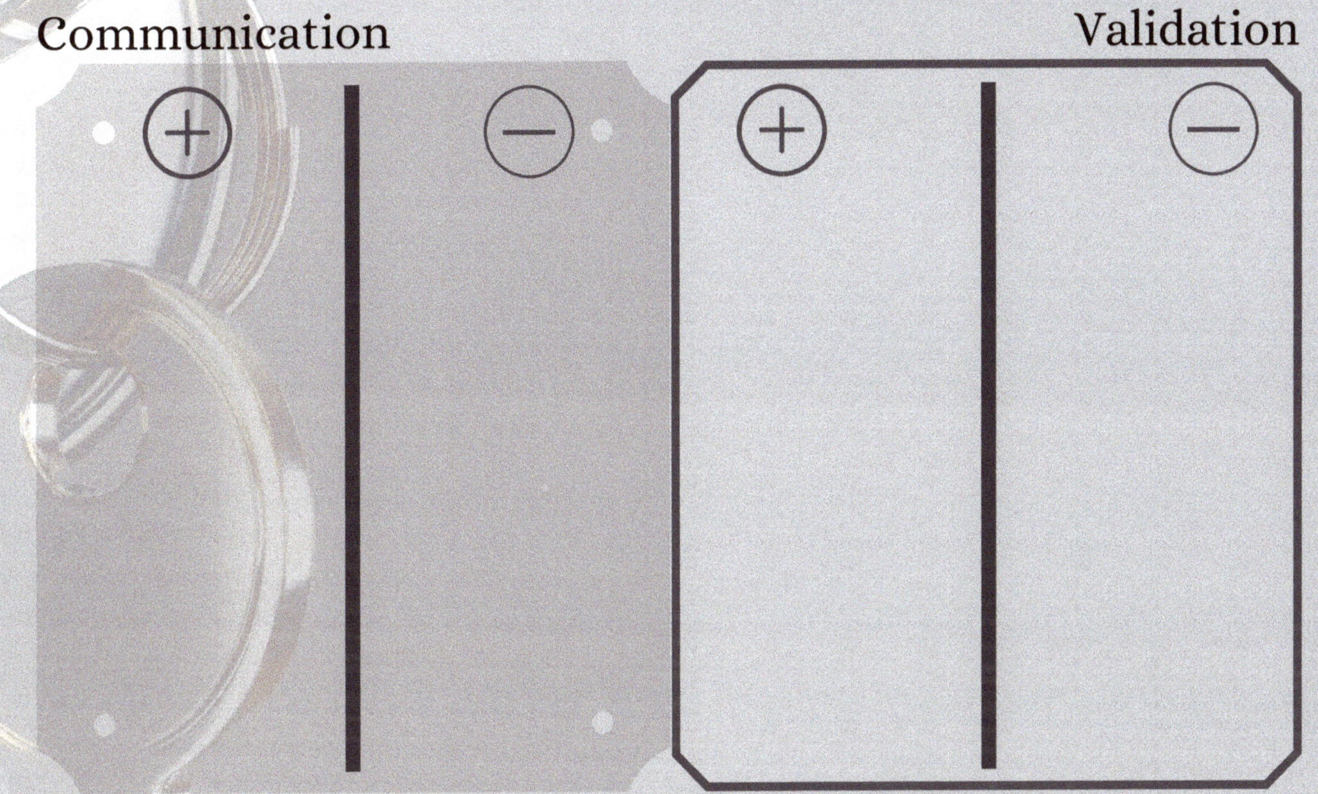

I would like to develop the following keys:

Day 1; Pt. 2- The Journey Begins: For Your Consideration

Read the prompts below and respond by filling each space provided with images and words that come into mind.

<table>
<tr><td>

I am most comfortable when....
& The happiest moments in life for me are:

</td><td>

Situations and things that make me uneasy:

</td></tr>
<tr><td>

I define peace as:

</td><td>

I define happiness as:

</td></tr>
</table>

Communication: Listening & Speaking

HOW WE EXPRESS OURSELVES WITH AND TO OTHERS IS AN IMPORTANT COMMUNICATION SKILL.

FINDING YOUR KEYS EMPHASIZES
THE IMPORTANCE OF LISTENING AND SPEAKING SKILLS WHEN COMMUNICATING.

Listening

Do you hear me? Are you listening to me?
Are you an effective listener?
Are you an active or passive listener?

One might say, *I hear you* or *I'm listening to you* and you might think they are saying the same thing but they are not, because **hearing** and **listening** are different:

- **Hearing** implies a distracted or involuntary action.
- **Listening** implies an engaged and intentional action.

Listening can be active or passive. Active versus Passive listening have different traits.

- **Active listening** requires engagement and participation.
- **Passive listing** occurs when you are distracted, lack focus and when the conversation is one sided.

When you are fully immersed in what the other person is saying, you can clearly communicate and convey engagement/understanding. Actively participating in a conversation without changing the focus, showing understanding or empathizing are **traits of an effective listener**.

How you receive(accept) what someone is saying, forms the foundation to how you "show" up for yourself and others.

DAY 2 LISTENING PRE-WORK

For Your Consideration

Are you a good listener?
List the attributes that make you a good listener and those you want to improve upon.
(this can be in general, daily, situational or when interacting with specific people.)

The qualities that make me a good listener:	In need to do the following things better to improve my listening skills:

"Shut Up"

AND JUST LISTEN

Not every great orator or person who checks yes to the question, "Do you have good communication skills?" actually communicates well.
In order to be a good communicator, sometimes you have to **Stop Talking** and **Just Listen**

Analyze your listening skills by completing the following:

Describe a situation when you didn't feel heard.

- How did you feel and what did you do?

Finish the following sentence: I listen best when I am:

I rate my listening: **Poor** 1 - 2 - 3 - 4 - 5 - 6 - 7 - 8 - 9 - 10 **Outstanding**

I would like to improve how I listen to others (example, boss, friend, co-worker, family member):

I will become an effective listener by improving my:

Over the next week actively work on your listening skills

Think

BEFORE YOU SPEAK

Once you say it out loud and others hear,
you can never truly take it back.
Unlike a typed message, the luxury of an
undo button is not available to erase what
you said.

People can forgive, but rarely do they Forget!

DAY4PT.1 – LISTENING ACTIVITY

For Your Consideration

I will remove distractions and acknowledge the person I am engaged in conversation with.

Signs to look for when I'm hearing but not listening:	How will I show that I'm listening:

Words I use to convey I'm Actively Listening:	Things I need to do ensure I'm actively listening:

For Your Consideration

Are you a good at communicating how you feel?
List the situations when you express your thoughts clearly and those you want to improve upon.
(this can be in general, daily, situational or when interacting with specific people.)

situations when I am able to articulate my thoughts clearly:

Situations where I feel my ability to articulate can improve:

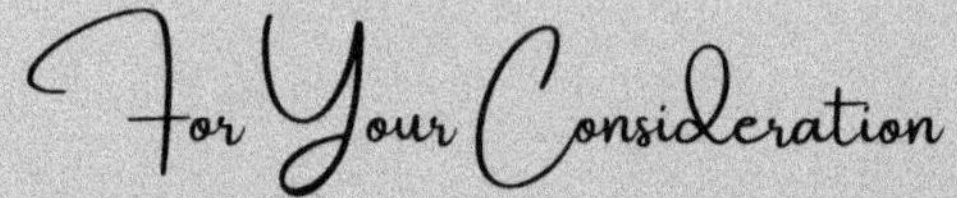

Thinking about your expectations use a recent conversation to answer:

Did I have the appropriate audience? Yes / No
(if No, why)

What was the purpose in starting the conversation?

Was I clear? Did they comprehend what I was trying to express?
Yes / No (if No, why)

How was the timing of the conversation, were there distractions?

Was I using active or passive listening skills?

Was the conversation effective? If no, why not? What was left
unsaid or not achieved?

What will you do differently?

Speaking

The art of self expression is important when exploring the root of your feelings on the journey to find peace and happiness.

Benefits of Expressing Yourself Effectively:
- People are able to experience the authentic and genuine you.
- You move from being a passive passenger on the journey to taking control of those things that happen in your life by becoming a contributor or driver.
- Doors are unlocked which allow you to establish effective boundaries while securing your emotional feelings.
- You begin to build confidence and self identity.

Provide an example of a recent conversation when someone wanted your feedback.

Use that scenario to respond the following:

Were you clear in your thoughts?   Yes   No

Were you supportive or judgmental? Yes   No

Describe how you were supportive

Describe how you were judgmental

How did you express empathy?

Everyone isn't worthy of your time, consideration or conversation.
First...

Check Credentials

Gassing others emotions, confidence, feelings or thinking up to the point they are on a false high for your own benefit or pleasure is not funny.

It's Dangerous!

Laughing gas should only be administered by a clinical professional.

Anything less just makes you look silly for believing the hype.

DAY 6 PT. 2 - COMMUNICATION ACTIVITY *For Your Consideration*

My best conversation yesterday was with ______________ about:

COMMUNICATION ACTIVITY PT. 3

I listen best when:

I feel heard when I talk to (_) because:

I feel most comfortable speaking when:

I find it easy to speak to (_) because:

ARE YOU LISTENING???

What do you want me to say?

If I say Yes, Do you feel heard?
If I say No, Are you offended?

The truth? Sometimes I am and other times I'm not.

Why? My mood or what's on my mind may be occupying too much space for me to engage fully.

I may not have the capacity to be present the way you need me to be.

The reason isn't about you, it's me. I've checked out, check back with me later!

Ask the Question:
Is this a good time to talk and for you to listen?

nmg

Reflect on a recent conversation that didn't go as planned. Why did you select that individual? What was the purpose/objective of the talk? Answer below...

Did I have the appropriate audience?

What was the purpose/objective in starting the conversation?

Was I clear? Did they comprehended what I was trying to express?

How was the timing of the conversation? Were their Distractions?

Was I using active or passive listening skills?

Why wasn't the conversation effective? How did I convey that?

Self Protection

Part of the journey to
Self-Love & Happiness
is understanding what you need and how
to express it **verbally**.
It all falls under the banner of
self-care.

**I AM NO LONGER BROKEN,
& I AM NOT YET WHOLE.**

I AM A WORK IN PROGRESS!

Stand Guard & Speak Up!

Rest Stop & Review

DATE:

The highlights of the week:

The struggles of the week:

The Lesson(s) I Learned:

This week I read the following book:

This week I tried for the first time:

My focus for the upcoming week will be:

Communication

<u>**You Have:**</u>

Examined how you communicate with others

Identified the ways others communicate with you

Evaluated your listening skills

Evaluated your speaking skills

Developed skills to help determine if you are opening up to the right people

Be Blessed

WHAT A TESTIMONY

Today may not have been a GREAT day, but you best believe it was a Blessed Day.

Don't let those things that didn't go your way be the instance(s) that determine your outcome or thinking.

That temporary situation will (and can't) have permanent residency.

Just know you *ARE* the blessing and no one can rob you of that fact!

nMS

Self-Reflection

Communication wrap-up

Starting today 5 things you will do differently when communicating with others:

1

2

3

4

5

Self-Reflection -Keys

What keys will you use to effectively communicate?

Communication

COMMUNICATION IS THE KEY TO SUCCESS
IN ALL PARTS OF LIFE.

Ask questions, listen & act accordingly.

When you are missing any piece of this, you don't
communicate well.

In the words of my sister, Dr. K Saunders:
Before you say anything,

Pray First!

Keep it real without the games, consider the impact
of your actions on others, then ask yourself,
Was I Clear or Do I Care?

*Peace &
Blessings*

Communication Notes

Communication Notes

Validation

RECOGNITION OR AFFIRMATION THAT A
PERSON, THEIR FEELINGS AND OPINIONS
ARE VALID AND WORTHWHILE.

Validation

<u>You will</u>

- Explore why you seek validation.

- Find value in your own opinion.

- Discover how seeking approval from others makes you feel.

Give examples of when you seek the approval of others

Faces

Don't take my facial expressions personally!

My face doesn't tell a story about how
I feel about you, it tells a story about
ME!

How am I feeling
happy, sad, simply emotionless,
confused, confident or conflicted?

It could be any or all of the above,
The emotions that come across my face
are reflections of how **I** feel,
it's not about **YOU**.

Look within

DON'T LOOK FOR
VALIDATION IN MY
FACE!

From whom do you seek acceptance? Why?

Stand *in your own* LIGHT

and in your own lane

The victory can only be claimed by the genuine person.

Imitators and copycats will not be able to show valid proof of identity to claim the ultimate prize.

Claim it! Own it! You are your own stamp of approval

For Your Consideration

How do you go about obtaining validation from others? Who do you choose and why?

I feel bad when I don't receive validation from: (list names and why)

If I don't receive validation from other's I loose confidence and it stops me? Yes/No/Sometimes Sometimes - Why?

The best compliment I ever received was from ___________ when they said:

Those I seek validation from impact my choices because?

I'm not everyone's

Cup of Tea!

But I know who I am. No need for
your Sugar, Honey, Ice or Truvia.

My blend of herbs, grown in rich
soil from the Motherland is pure
and cultivated for that person
who desires the savory dark
smooth blend called

Me

nmS

DAY 13 VALIDATION

For Your Consideration

When I don't receive acceptance or approval from others that I expected, I react by:

What role(s) do those you seek acceptance play in your life (spouse, family, friend, boss, co-worker, acquaintance, customer, spiritual advisor)?:

Do you find those individuals supportive or envious of your success or growth? What actions have you observed that helped you determine if they they are Team You or Team Self when seeking feedback?

Delayed is not Denied

STOP
OVERTHINKING &
OVER REACTING
TO EVERYTHING & EVERYONE

Your peace is yours to:
find, keep or lose.

Remind yourself regularly because
it's easy to turn the controls over
to someone else.

DAY 14 VALIDATION

For Your Consideration

I seek guidance, council or therapy: Yes / No (past or present)

If Yes from: clergy, clinical/licensed individual, friend, family or other:_____________

I seek the help from them because or I don't seek help because:

Are your choices in alignment with what HE spiritually has laid on your heart?

Relationships Yes /No

Professional Work: Yes / No

Family: Yes / No

How does His confirmation / recomendation manifest?

Those you seek validation from, are you equally yoked?

Relationship(s):Yes / No

Professional Work: Yes / No

Family: Yes / No

Do they have experience in what you strive to do, or are they not at level to really lend support in helping you vet your decision or idea?

A WORD FOR YOU

Say Ouch

In the words of Neicy Nash, "If you can't say Amen, Say Ouch"

When something hits you a little differently and you are not ready for an embrace of the word delivered or you're still in denial, but YOU know it hit a little too close for comfort, it's okay to say

"Ouch"

God is patient and He is working on you. In due time you will welcome that word and embrace it with an "Amen". Then let it use you and put you in a position to respond differently.
He is waiting for you to listen, in the meantime..

Say, "Ouch"!

WMS

Rest Stop & Review

The highlights of the week:

The struggles of the week:

The Lesson(s) I Learned:

This week I read the following book:

This week I tried for the first time:

My focus for the upcoming week will be:

Validation

<u>You have evaluated:</u>

Reasons others acceptance is important.

How to identify when to seek validation from others vs. relying on your own opinion.

From whom & when to seek approval from others.

The importance of putting into context the feedback of others in comparison of your own feelings.

Why seeking validation isn't always bad.

Self-Reflection
Day 16 - Validation

Starting today 5 things you will do differently in search of validation

1

2

3

4

5

Self-Reflection

Day 16 - Validation

Self-Reflection -Keys

What were your self awareness moments when evaluating your desire for acceptance and approval from others?

LET IT FLOW..

Brush off your shoulders

When you know people are gunning for you
What do you do?
Still rise and tell them to:

Mind 'Ya Own Business!!

NMS

THE WEEK THAT WAS

Choose one word to best describe each day of the week.

After reflecting on your word choices, write a few sentences to sum up your week.

____
____
____
____
____
____

Validation Notes

Validation Notes

Happiness
& Peace

Happiness & Peace

<u>You will:</u>

- Determine what brings you happiness and peace.
- Identify those things that distract you from achieving Happiness and Peace.
- Use the skills developed in prior segments (communication and validation) to identify and articulate when your happiness or peace is being disrupted.
- Develop ways to constructively shut down conversations that aren't impacting you positively.
- Discover new Keys and Life Lessons.
  - Read or listen to a book (or two) that will help you grow. (see reference list)
  - Explore new things you have always wanted to do.

Enjoy the journey!

Ask yourself, what makes me happy and when am I at peace?

Happiness

I felt joy or pleasure when:

Peace

I felt calm and focused when:

I didn't feel Happy or Peace today when:

DO YOU WANT

Happiness?

DO YOU WANT

Peace?

Are you Happy?

This is a question that can't be answered with a simple Yes or No. It's more complex than a one syllable response. You can be happy with parts of your life and still not be truly *HAPPY*

Are you at Peace?

Peace is a level of acceptance and contentment that marks a point and place in your life. It allows you to be in a place of calm and focus like no other.

It's okay to seek both!

Happiness is relative, Peace is tangible.

Know what you're seeking

Ask yourself, what makes me happy and when am I at peace?

Happiness
I felt joy or pleasure when:

Peace
I felt calm and focused when:

I didn't feel Happy or at Peace today when:

Free Your Mind

AND THE REST WILL FLOW

It's FREE:

To Dream

To Create

To Realize your Destiny

Happiness and Peace..

they are yours for the taking.

You hold the Keys:

Unlock what Happiness and

Peace feels like to

YOU!

Ask yourself, what makes me happy and when am I at peace?

Happiness
I felt joy or pleasure when:

Peace
I felt calm and focused when:

I didn't feel Happy or at Peace today when:

Excellence...

- isn't about being perfect. It's about making a choice
- you choose to be the best version of you
- you work hard
- you give your best to all you do
- you speak your truth with grace and humility
- you walk in Love
- you lift others and help when you can
- you are at peace with the choices you make
- you do the right thing
- you go high when it's easy to go low
- you are a village

Be an example of

Excellence

Ask yourself, what makes me happy and when am I at peace?

Happiness
I felt joy or pleasure when:

Peace
I felt calm and focused when:

I didn't feel Happy or at Peace today when:

It is What It is!

It's not easy to accept things that aren't what you planned for in your day or life.

Just know you are the author of your own confusion because God has already written the plan and when you ignore His teachings you get stuck, hurt or set-back. Just live in the space of:

It is what It is & Trust His Will

Meditate and discern what He is saying to you, "Move child, GET OUT THE WAY" of our Father's plan for you.

NMS

Ask yourself, what makes me happy and when am I at peace?

Happiness
I felt joy or pleasure when:

Peace
I felt calm and focused when:

I didn't feel Happy or at Peace today when:

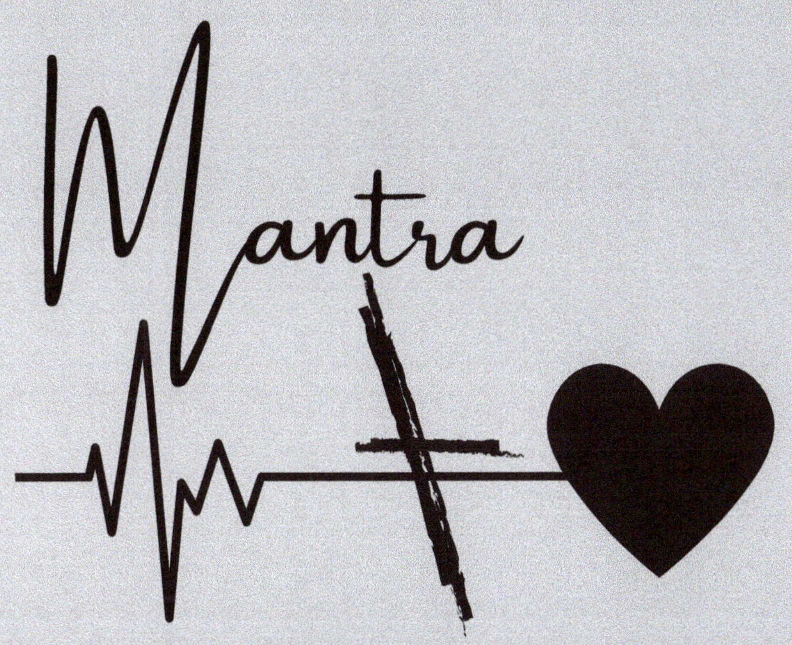

My Heart, Faith & Love
is unwavering &
it will get me through it all

Keep pushing even when it "seems" to
be overwhelming

NMS

Rest Stop & Review

The highlights of the week:

The struggles of the week:

The Lesson(s) I Learned:

This week I read the following book:

This week I tried for the first time:

My focus for the upcoming week will be:

Keep Running

DON'T GIVE UP

When you feel:
*Dread *Down *Depressed *Defeated
*Discouraged

The race isn't over until you finish

Keep pushing 'cause your purpose and
mission are already written.
When you can't run, walk!
One step at a time, keep the faith
and don't give up, I've got you, but
best of all;

God's Got You!

NMS

THE WEEK THAT WAS

Choose one word to best describe each day of the week.

After reflecting on your word choices, write a few sentences to sum up your week.

You are His

Masterpiece!

Inspirational, Intelligent Imagery that
Inspires others to be great!

No matter who you are,
don't quit & shine in whatever
you do.

Be the light & magic for
someone else who is looking for
inspiration.

Be an example of achievement.
You are that light & love for the
next one!
You are Art!
NMS

Ask yourself, what makes me happy and when am I at peace?

Happiness
I felt joy or pleasure when:

Peace
I felt calm and focused when:

I didn't feel Happy or at Peace today when:

DON'T LET ANYONE STEER YOU OFF OF THE

path God has set for you

IN EXCHANGE FOR THE PROMISE OF RICHES AND GOLD.

No one has ever found <u>true</u> love and comfort in material things.

If they tell you they did, just know that DEVIL is a Liar!

Recognize before it's too late
Make a U-Turn to get back on the path
of **God.**

For Your Consideration

Ask yourself, what makes me happy and when am I at peace?

Happiness
I felt joy or pleasure when:

Peace
I felt calm and focused when:

I didn't feel Happy or at Peace today when:

Walk in Love

When in doubt, feeling wronged,
misunderstood, overlooked, unheard, hurt or
unfairly judged.

Remember Love heals all wounds and builds the
bridge to unity, forgiveness, clarity and wholeness.

Walk in love for we all have made mistakes,
done wrong and sought redemption.
We are humans living a life and learning as we go.

Take the path of Love
and show others how it's done!

NMS

Ask yourself, what makes me happy and when am I at peace?

Happiness
I felt joy or pleasure when:

Peace
I felt calm and focused when:

I didn't feel Happy or at Peace today when:

Cast Away the Critics

Do what you can to
put forth your best
effort

Do not let anyone
negatively judge your
efforts

Focus on the Walk
& not the Talk

NMS

Ask yourself, what makes me happy and when am I at peace?

Happiness
I felt joy or pleasure when:

Peace
I felt calm and focused when:

I didn't feel Happy or at Peace today when:

Get back UP!

IF YOU STUMBLE OR FALL,

GET UP
CATCH YOUR BALANCE AND KEEP PUSHING

Failure is not
in your vocabulary.

Find your motivation and
keep moving toward.
Find your Keys!

Self-Reflection

Day 28 - Happiness & Peace wrap-up

Starting today 5 things you will do differently

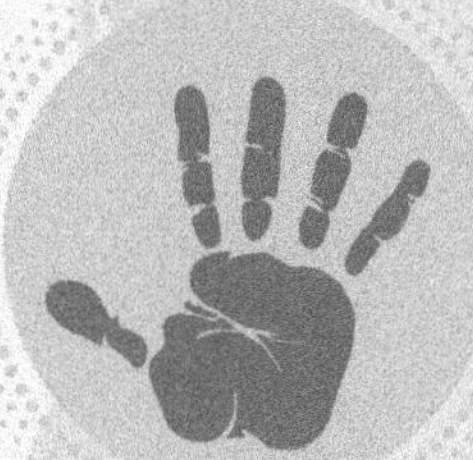

1

2

3

4

5

Self-Reflection - Keys

Day 28 - Happiness & Peace wrap-up

What were your self awareness moments on the journey to finding Happiness and Peace?

Recognizing the Skills & Keys

Communication is the key to success in all parts of your life.

Ask questions, listen and act accordingly. When you are missing any piece of this, you don't communicate well.

Prayer first!

Keep it real without the games, consider the impact of your actions on others.

Ask yourself:

WAS I CLEAR OR DO I CARE?

Rest Stop & Review

The highlights of the week:

The struggles of the week:

The Lesson(s) I Learned:

This week I read the following book:

This week I tried for the first time:

My focus for the upcoming week will be:

The journey

IS YOURS TO TAKE!

Peace and Happiness are found when you say YES to those things you are afraid of failing and to those things you always wanted to do.

The Key:

God has written your story. You are the director and producer of how your story is told.

Don't let others fool you into believing anything different.

Day 30 The End of the Journey

You are at the end of this journey, what did this process teach you about yourself?

What are your next steps to protect your Happiness and Peace?

What habits will you continue to do?

Pt. 2: The Journey Ends: For Your Consideration

Revisit part of your first assignment. Read the prompts below and respond by filling each space provided with images and words that come into mind based on what you've learned on this journey.

I am most comfortable when....
& The happiest moments in life for me:

Situations and things that make me uneasy:

I define peace as:

I define happiness as:

Happiness & Peace

Today I promise to continue to:

- Be a good listener
- Listen and speak effectively
- Look within for my validation before seeking it from others
- Be selective from who I seek guidance
- Acknowledge that happiness and peace are mine to lock and protect

My journey isn't over and I will continue to find happiness and peace daily.

Sincerely,

____

Conclusion

You have completed the 30 day journey to finding your KEYS.

Are you able to answer the five questions asked in the introduction differently?

1. Am I an effective communicator?
2. Do I surrender my communication power to others?
3. Do I provide others with Keys to lock or unlock your peace and happiness?
4. Are my choices bringing me peace and happiness?
5. Do the choices I make aid in the advancement of the success of others, their survival and happiness ahead of my own?"

My prayer for you is that you have found your Keys to unlock your voice, self empowerment and those things that bring you true happiness and peace. When you feel you've lost any of them, review what you've written.

Let this serve as a map to locating them. Continue to explore what brings you joy and exercise your voice when you are unclear about the intentions of others or when they are attempting to steal your Keys.

Now that you've found your keys, keep hold of them and always remind yourself that you hold the passcode to the lockbox that you store those keys in. It's up to you if you decide to unlock it.

The last exercise is to create that passcode.

Hold it tight and don't forget it!

Securing Your Keys – The final exercise
Creating a Lockbox Passcode

THE KEYS OPENED THE FOLLOWING DOORS:

What I Learned about- **My Communication**	What I learned about- **Validation**	What brings me: **Happiness & Peace**

Happiness & Peace Notes

Happiness & Peace Notes

Happiness & Peace Notes

Reference Materials

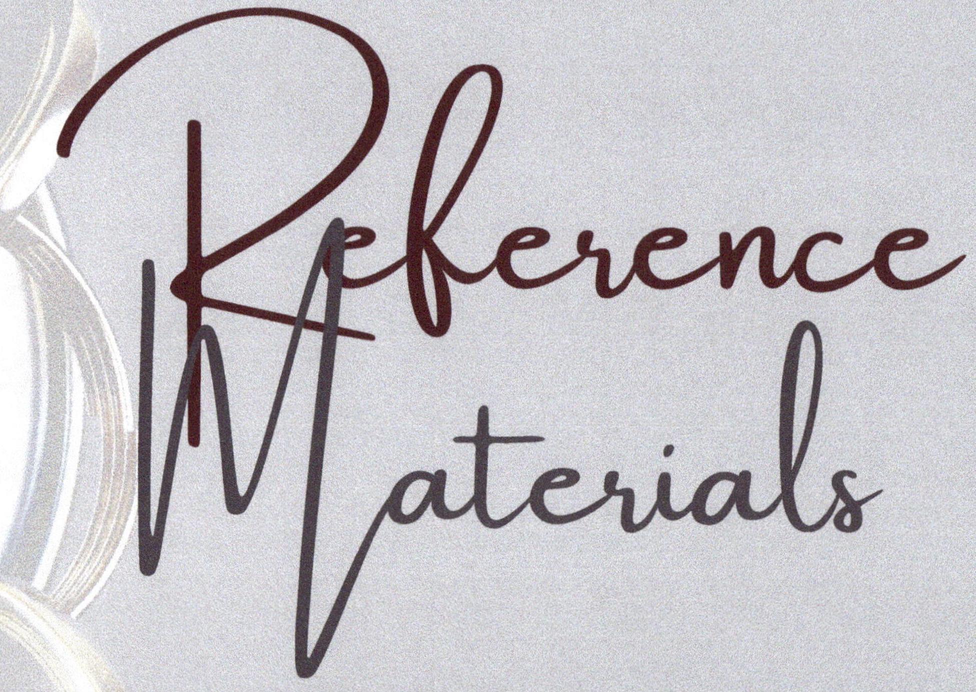

Reference Materials

Definitions:

Operational descriptions for interpretational purposes as you travel on your journey.

Books:

Suggestions that helped me when I explored this journey.

They are all available in paper and audio versions for your reading and listening pleasures.

Definitions

journey noun - something suggesting travel or passage from one place to another

key noun- a: extremely or crucially important; b: the set of instructions governing the encipherment and decipherment of messages; c: a means of gaining or preventing entrance, possession, or control

happy adjective - enjoying or characterized by well-being and contentment

happiness noun - a state of well-being and contentment
b : a pleasurable or satisfying experience

peace noun - harmony in personal relations;: a state of tranquility or quiet

validation noun - recognition or affirmation that a person or their feelings or opinions are valid or worthwhile.

validate verb - recognize or affirm the validity or worth of (a person or their feelings or opinions); cause (a person) to feel valued or worthwhile.

purpose noun - the reason for which something is done or created or for which something exists.

communication noun - the imparting or exchanging of information or news.

engage verb - (engage with) establish a meaningful contact or connection with.

Yoke verb - (equally yoked) the connection or cause (for two people) to be joined in a personal relationship, work or situation.

Book Suggestions

This is a list of books (in no particular order) I found helpful along my journey of self discovery and improvement. I encourage you to never stop learning and working on yourself. Read a book, take a seminar, listen about how others do it, it may unlock something in you. All of the below books are also available on audio as well:

- **The Power of I Am: Two Words That Will Change Your Life Today** - By: Joel Osteen
- **The Five Love Languages -** By: Gary Chapman
- **Year of Yes: How to Dance It Out, Stand in the Sun and Be Your Own Person** - By: Shonda Rhimes
- **Lioness Arising: Wake Up and Change Your World** - By: Lisa Bevere
- **Wholeness: Winning in Life from the Inside Out** - By: Touré Roberts
- **Believe Bigger: Discover the Path to Your Life Purpose** - By: Marshawn Evans Daniels
- **Abundance Now: Amplify Your Life & Achieve Prosperity Today** - By: Lisa Nichols
- **Crucial Conversations: Tools for Talking When Stakes Are High, Second Edition** - By: Kerry Patterson
- **The Four Agreements** - By: don Miguel Ruiz
- **It's Not What It Looks Like -** By: Molly Burke
- **UnOffendable** - By: Ryan Leak
- **Essentialism: The Disciplined Pursuit of Less** - By: Greg McKeown
- **Discerning the Voice of God; How to recognize when God speaks** - By: Priscilla Shirer
- **The 7 Habits of Highly Effective People** - By: Stephen R. Covey
- **Living a Life You Love** - By: Joyce Meyer

Happiness & Peace Notes

Happiness & Peace Notes

Forever
KS

Dedicated to the membery of Dr. K
Kimberly Saunders

THANK YOU FOR PURCHASING THIS
JOURNAL AND EXERCISE BOOK,
WRITTEN WITH THE EXPRESSED
INTENT OF HELPING THE NEXT
PERSON FIND THEIR KEYS.

NEVER LET YOUR VOICE BE
SILENCED.

#BExpressive

www.ingramcontent.com/pod-product-compliance
Lightning Source LLC
Chambersburg PA
CBHW040906130726
48005CB00019BA/2994